THE WARFARE
OF THE CHURCHES

Tozer's Very Last Message to the Church
(*Printed 2 days after his death*)

Author of FIVE VOWS OF SPIRITUAL POWER;
GOD STILL SPEAKS; HOW TO BE FILLED WITH THE HOLY SPIRIT;
BORN AFTER MIDNIGHT, etc., etc.

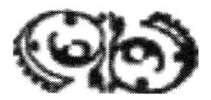

CHRISTIAN AND MISSIONARY ALLIANCE
Nyack, New York
1963

Scripture taken from
The Holy Bible: King James Version

PLEASE SEE THE BACK PAGE FOR MORE GREAT TITLES
AVAILABLE THROUGH CROSSREACH PUBLICATIONS.
AND IF YOU ENJOYED THIS BOOK PLEASE CONSIDER LEAVING A
REVIEW ON AMAZON. THAT HELPS US OUT A LOT. THANKS.

CROSSREACH
PUBLICATIONS
AVAILABLE IN PAPERBACK AND EBOOK EDITIONS
© 2016 CROSSREACH PUBLICATIONS
ALL RIGHTS RESERVED, INCLUDING THE RIGHT TO REPRODUCE
THIS BOOK OR PORTIONS THEREOF IN ANY FORM WHATEVER.

THE WANING AUTHORITY OF CHRIST IN THE CHURCHES

Here is the burden of my heart; and while I claim for myself no special inspiration I yet feel that this is also the burden of the Spirit.

If I know my own heart it is love alone that moves me to write this. What I write here is not the sour ferment of a mind agitated by contentions with my fellow Christians. There have been no such contentions. I have not been abused, mistreated or attacked by anyone. Nor have these observations grown out of any unpleasant experiences that I have had in my association with others. My relations with my own church as well as with Christians of other denominations have been friendly, courteous and pleasant. My grief is simply the result of a condition which I believe to be almost universally prevalent among the churches.

I think also that I should acknowledge that I am myself very much involved in the situation I here deplore. As Ezra in his mighty prayer of intercession included himself among the wrongdoers, so do I. "O my God, I am ashamed and blush to lift up my face to thee, my God: for our iniquities are increased over our head, and our trespass is grown up unto the heavens." Any hard word spoken here against others must in simple honesty return upon my own head. I too have been guilty. This is written with the hope that we all may turn unto the Lord our God and sin no more against Him.

Let me state the cause of my burden. It is this: Jesus Christ has today almost no authority at all among the groups that call themselves by His name. By these I mean not the Roman Catholics nor the liberals, nor the various quasi-Christian cults. I do mean Protestant churches generally, and I include those that protest the loudest that they are in spiritual descent from our Lord and His apostles, namely, the evangelicals.

It is a basic doctrine of the New Testament that after His resurrection the Man Jesus was declared by God to be both Lord and Christ, and that He was invested by the Father with absolute Lordship over the church which is His Body. All authority is His in heaven and in earth. In His own proper time He will exert it to the full, but during this period in history He allows this authority to be challenged or ignored. And just now it is being challenged by the world and ignored by the church.

The present position of Christ in the gospel churches may be likened to that of a king in a limited, constitutional monarchy. The king (sometimes depersonalized by the term "the Crown") is in such a country no more than a traditional rallying point, a pleasant symbol of unity and loyalty much like a flag or a national anthem. He is lauded, feted and supported, but his real authority is small. Nominally he is head over all, but in every crisis someone else makes the decisions. On formal occasions he appears in his royal attire to deliver the tame, colorless speech put into his mouth by the real rulers of the country. The whole thing may be no more than good-natured make-believe, but it is rooted in antiquity, it is a lot of fun and no one wants to give it up.

Among the gospel churches Christ is now in fact little more than a beloved symbol. "All Hail the Power of Jesus' Name" is the church's national anthem and the cross is her official flag, but in the week-by-week services of the church and the day-by-day conduct of her members someone else, not Christ, makes the decisions. Under proper circumstances Christ is allowed to say "Come unto me, all ye that labour and are heavy laden" or "Let not your heart be troubled," but when the speech is finished someone else takes over. Those in actual authority decide the moral standards of the church, as well as all objectives and all methods employed to achieve them. Because of long and meticulous organization it is now possible for the youngest pastor just out of seminary to have more actual authority in a church than Jesus Christ has.

Not only does Christ have little or no authority; His influence also is becoming less and less. I would not say that He has none, only that it is small and diminishing. A fair parallel would be the influence of Abraham Lincoln over the American people. Honest Abe is still the idol of the country. The likeness of his kind, rugged face, so homely that it is beautiful, appears everywhere. It is easy to grow misty-eyed over him. Children are brought up on stories of his love, his honesty and his humility.

But after we have gotten control over our tender emotions what have we left? No more than a good example which, as it recedes into the past, becomes more and more unreal and exercises less and less real influence. Every scoundrel is ready to wrap Lincoln's long black coat around him. In the cold light of political facts in the United States the constant appeal to Lincoln by the politicians is a cynical joke.

The Lordship of Jesus is not quite forgotten among Christians, but it has been relegated to the hymnal where all responsibility toward it may be comfortably discharged in a glow of pleasant religious emotion. Or if it is taught as a theory in the classroom it is rarely applied to practical living. The idea that the Man Christ Jesus has absolute and final authority over the whole church and over all of its members in every detail of their lives is simply not now accepted as true by the rank and file of evangelical Christians.

What we do is this: We accept the Christianity of our group as being identical with that of Christ and His apostles. The beliefs, the practices, the ethics, the activities of our group are equated with the Christianity of the New Testament. Whatever the group thinks or says or does is scriptural, no questions asked. It is assumed that all our Lord expects of us is that we busy ourselves with the activities of the group. In so doing we are keeping the commandments of Christ.

To avoid the hard necessity of either obeying or rejecting the plain instructions of our Lord in the New Testament we take refuge in a liberal interpretation of them. Casuistry is not the possession of Roman Catholic theologians alone. We evangelicals also know how to avoid the sharp point of obedience by means of fine and intricate explanations. These are tailor-made for the flesh. They excuse disobedience, comfort carnality and make the words of Christ of none effect. And the essence of it all is that Christ simply could not have meant what He said. His teachings are accepted even theoretically only after they have been weakened by interpretation.

Yet Christ is consulted by increasing numbers of persons with "problems" and sought after by those who long for peace of mind. He is widely recommended as a kind of spiritual psychiatrist with remarkable powers to straighten people out. He is able to deliver them from their guilt complexes and to help them to avoid serious psychic traumas by making a smooth and easy adjustment to society and to their own ids. Of course this strange Christ has no relation whatever to the Christ of the New Testament. The true Christ is also Lord, but this accommodating Christ is little more than the servant of the people.

But I suppose I should offer some concrete proof to support my charge that Christ has little or no authority today among the churches. Well, let me put a few questions and let the answers be the evidence.

Waning Authority of Christ

What church board consults our Lord's words to decide matters under discussion? Let anyone reading this who has had experience on a church board try to recall the times or time when any board member read from the Scriptures to make a point, or when any chairman suggested that the brethren should see what instructions the Lord had for them on a particular question. Board meetings are habitually opened with a formal prayer or "a season of prayer"; after that the Head of the Church is respectfully silent while the real rulers take over. Let anyone who denies this bring forth evidence to refute it. I for one will be glad to hear it.

What Sunday school committee goes to the Word for directions? Do not the members invariably assume that they already know what they are supposed to do and that their only problem is to find effective means to get it done? Plans, rules, "operations" and new methodological techniques absorb all their time and attention. The prayer before the meeting is for divine help to carry out their plans. Apparently the idea that the Lord might have some instructions for them never so much as enters their heads.

Who remembers when a conference chairman brought his Bible to the table with him for the purpose of using it? Minutes, regulations, rules of order, yes. The sacred commandments of the Lord, no. An absolute dichotomy exists between the devotional period and the business session. The first has no relation to the second.

What foreign mission board actually seeks to follow the guidance of the Lord as provided by His Word and His Spirit? They all think they do, but what they do in fact is to assume the scripturalness of their ends and then ask for help to find ways to achieve them. They may pray all night for God to give success to their enterprises, but Christ is desired as their helper, not as their Lord. Human means

Waning Authority of Christ

are devised to achieve ends assumed to be divine. These harden into policy, and thereafter the Lord doesn't even have a vote.

In the conduct of our public worship where is the authority of Christ to be found? The truth is that today the Lord rarely controls a service, and the influence He exerts is very small. We sing of Him and preach about Him, but He must not interfere; we worship our way, and it must be right because we have always done it that way, as have the other churches in our group.

What Christian when faced with a moral problem goes straight to the Sermon on the Mount or other New Testament Scripture for the authoritative answer? Who lets the words of Christ be final on giving, birth control, the bringing up of a family, personal habits, tithing, entertainment, buying, selling and other such important matters?

What theological school, from the lowly Bible institute up, could continue to operate if it were to make Christ Lord of its every policy? There may be some, and I hope there are, but I believe I am right when I say that most such schools" to stay in business are forced to adopt procedures which find no justification in the Bible they profess to teach. So we have this strange anomaly: the authority of Christ is ignored in order to maintain a school to teach among other things the authority of Christ.

The causes back of the decline in our Lord's authority are many. I name only two.

One is the power of custom, precedent and tradition within the older religious groups. These like gravitation affect every particle of religious practice within the group, exerting a steady and constant pressure in one direction. Of course that direction is toward conformity to the status quo. Not Christ but custom is lord in this situation. And the same thing has passed over (possibly to a slightly lesser degree) into the other groups such as the full gospel tabernacles, the holiness churches, the pentecostal and fundamental churches and the many independent and undenominational churches found everywhere throughout the North American continent.

The second cause is the revival of intellectualism among the evangelicals. This, if I sense the situation correctly, is not so much a thirst for learning as a desire for a reputation of being learned. Because of it good men who ought to know better are being put in the position of collaborating with the enemy. I'll explain.

Our evangelical faith (which I believe to be the true faith of Christ and His apostles) is being attacked these days from many different directions. In the Western world the enemy has forsworn violence. He comes against us no more with sword and fagot; he now comes smiling, bearing gifts.

He raises his eyes to heaven and swears that he too believes in the faith of our fathers, but his real purpose is to destroy that faith, or at least to modify it to such an extent that it is no longer the supernatural thing it once was. He comes in the name of philosophy or psychology or anthropology, and with sweet reasonableness urges us to rethink our historic position, to be less rigid, more tolerant, more broadly understanding.

He speaks in the sacred jargon of the schools, and many of our half-educated evangelicals run to fawn on him. He tosses academic degrees to the scrambling sons of the prophets as Rockefeller used to toss dimes to the children of the peasants. The evangelicals who, with some justification, have been accused of lacking true scholarship, now grab for these status symbols with shining eyes, and when they get them they are scarcely able to believe their eyes. They walk about in a kind of ecstatic unbelief, much as the soloist of the neighborhood church choir might were she to be invited to sing at La Scala.

For the true Christian the one supreme test for the present soundness and ultimate worth of everything religious must be the place our Lord occupies in it. Is He Lord or symbol? Is He in charge of the project or merely one of the crew? Does He decide things or only help to carry out the plans of others? All religious activities, from the simplest act of an individual Christian to the ponderous and expensive operations of a whole denomination, may be proved by the answer to the question, Is Jesus Christ Lord in this act? Whether our works prove to be wood, hay and stubble or gold and silver and precious stones in that great day will depend upon the right answer to that question.

What, then, are we to do? Each one of us must decide, and there are at least three possible choices. One is to rise up in shocked indignation and accuse me of irresponsible reporting. Another is to nod general agreement with what is written here but take comfort in the fact that there are exceptions and we are among the exceptions. The other is to go down in meek humility and confess that we have grieved the Spirit and dishonored our Lord in failing to give Him the place His Father has given Him as Head and Lord of the Church.

Either the first or the second will but confirm the wrong. The third if carried out to its conclusion can remove the curse. The decision lies with us.

About CrossReach Publications

Thank you for choosing CrossReach Publications.

Our philosophy is to remain as neutral as possible. We are non-denominational and non-sectarian. We seek to publish books from a wide variety of authors and doctrinal positions, on a wide variety of Christian topics that will teach, encourage, challenge, inspire and equip. We appreciate and respect what every part of the body brings to the table and believe everyone has the right to study and come to their own conclusions. *We aim to help to facilitate that end.*

We aspire to excellence. If we have not met your standards please contact us and let us know. We want you to feel satisfied with your product. Amy, our 11 year old, has recently joined the business now and is publishing her own books. And Sarah, our 5 year old, loves to mimic daddy "doing the books"!
We're a family-based home-business. A husband and wife team raising 8 kids. You can see us in action in our family vlog. If you have any questions or comments about our publications or our channel you can do so by emailing us.

www.YouTube.com/c/TheKinsellaBunchVlog
CrossReach@outlook.com
Don't forget you can follow us on Facebook and Twitter, and keep up to date on our newest releases and deals.

Also from CrossReach Publications

How to Be Filled with the Holy Spirit
A. W. Tozer

Before we deal with the question of how to be filled with the Holy Spirit, there are some matters which first have to be settled. As believers you have to get them out of the way, and right here is where the difficulty arises. I have been afraid that my listeners might have gotten the idea somewhere that I had a how-to-be-filled-with-the-Spirit-in-five-easy-lessons doctrine, which I could give you. If you can have any such vague ideas as that, I can only stand before you and say, "I am sorry"; because it isn't true; I can't give you such a course. There are some things, I say, that you have to get out of the way, settled.

God Still Speaks
A. W. Tozer

Tozer is as popular today as when he was living on the earth. He is respected right across the spectrum of Christianity, in circles that would disagree sharply with him doctrinally. Why is this? A. W. Tozer was a man who knew the voice of God. He shared this experience with every true child of God. With all those who are called by the grace of God to share in the mystical union that is possible with Him through His Son Jesus.

Tozer fought against much dryness and formality in his day. Considered a mighty man of God by most Evangelicals today, he was unconventional in his approach to spirituality and had no qualms about consulting everyone from Catholic Saints to

German Protestant mystics for inspiration on how to experience God more fully.

Tozer, just like his Master, doesn't fit neatly into our theological boxes. He was a man after God's own heart and was willing to break the rules (man-made ones that is) to get there.

Here are two writings by Tozer that touch on the heart of this goal. Revelation is Not Enough and The Speaking Voice. A bonus chapter The Menace of the Religious Movie is included.

This is meat to sink your spiritual teeth into. Tozer's writings will show you the way to satisfy your spiritual hunger.
—Dave Kinsella

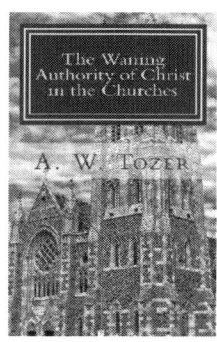

The Waning Authority of Christ in the Churches
A. W. Tozer

This book has been described by James L. Snyder as Tozer's valedictory. It was his last message ever given to God's people. Written shortly before his death in 1963, it was published two days after his death. It is a challenging message to all who want to walk with Christ.

"HERE IS THE BURDEN of my heart; and while I claim for myself no special inspiration I yet feel that this is also the burden of the Spirit. If I know my own heart it is love alone that moves me to write this. What I write here is not the sour ferment of a mind agitated by contentions with my fellow Christians. There have been no such contentions. I have not been abused, mistreated or attacked by anyone. Nor have these observations grown out of any unpleasant experiences that I have had in my association with others. My relations with my own church as well as with Christians of other denominations have been friendly, courteous and pleasant. My grief is simply the result of a condition which I believe to be almost universally prevalent among the churches."

Born After Midnight
A. W. Tozer

To speak to God on behalf of men is probably the highest service any of us can render. The next is to speak to men in the name of God. Either is a privilege possible to us only through the grace of our Lord Jesus Christ. To sit even for a moment in the chair of the teacher and write that which may affect the life and character of numerous persons is not only a lofty privilege but a grave responsibility as well. The only qualifications I bring to the writing of these pages are love for the Triune Godhead and a sorrowful concern for the spiritual welfare of the Church which our Lord purchased with His own blood. If there is anything here good or helpful to the children of God it must be attributed to the operation of the Holy Spirit who often condescends to work through unworthy instruments. Whatever else may be found here is due to human weakness and is better forgotten. My prayers go with this book and with all who may chance to read it.

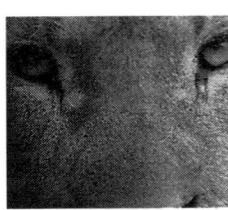

Five Vows of Spiritual Power
A. W. Tozer

Some people object to taking vows, but in the Bible you will find many great men of God directed by covenants, promises, vows and pledges. The psalmist was not averse to the taking of vows: "Thy vows are upon me, O God," he said. "I will render my praises unto thee" (Psalm 56:12).

My counsel in this matter is that if you are really concerned about spiritual improvement—the gaining of new power, new life, new joy and new personal revival within your heart—you will do well to make certain vows and proceed to keep them. If you should fail, go down in humility and repent and start over. But always keep these vows before you. They will help harmonize your heart with the vast powers that flow out and down from the throne where Christ sits at the right hand of God.

Let My People Go: The Life of Robert A. Jaffray
A. W. Tozer

Robert A. Jaffray was a citizen of no single country. From his early manhood he moved about over the face of the world—not aimlessly, but with clear intelligent purpose. He was an explorer, a pioneer, and this accounts for the gaps that will be found in this or any story of his life. He lived in too many places too far from each other to allow a closely woven biography to be written. One could have journeyed half way around the world to see him, only to find that he had left the day before to visit some remote point in the Far East where some important gathering looked to him for guidance.

Wingspread: The Life of A. B. Simpson
A. W. Tozer

Any man who has reason to hope (or to fear) that someone may someday write the story of his life would do well to pray that he may not fall into the hand of an enemy, a disciple, a rival or a relative.
Of all men, these make the poorest biographers. Their relationship to the subject places them where they cannot see him as he actually is, so the picture they paint, however interesting it may be, is never true to the original.

The best biographer comes from a far country. He can see the subject as he is, and being free from the handicap of a close personal relation, he will, if he have a fair amount of intelligence and enough patience to make himself familiar with the facts, be in a position to present a reasonably accurate picture of what he sees.

Paths to Power
A. W. Tozer

We present in these pages an outline, which may at least serve to suggest the way to a greater spiritual power for many of us. Or, as the title intimates, each major idea may be a "path" leading to a life of abundant grace promised in the Sacred Word. Let us remember that a path is merely a way toward something; it can never be the thing itself. A knowledge of the truth is not enough; the truth must be followed if we would realize in actual experience the blessedness which is here described.

In Defense of Parents
A. W. Tozer

Well, for many years now we Americans have had a convenient culprit upon which to blame just about everything. Or rather we have had a whole flock of them, for their name is Legion, and they are charged with a variety of psychological crimes, all of which are within the law as it stands but are destructive and antisocial nevertheless and indirectly the cause of gang fights, rapes, juvenile delinquency, child desertion. dope addiction, embezzlement, switch blade murders, rock and roll hysteria, strong-arm robbery and drunkenness. And who are they? Parents. Yes, sir, Mother and Dad are responsible for all these things.

The Praying Plumber of Lisburn
A. W. Tozer

Tom Haire is a rare compound of deep, tender devotion, amazing good sense and a delightful sense of humor. There is about him absolutely nothing of the tension found in so many persons who seek to live the spiritual life.

Tom is completely free in the Spirit and will not allow himself to be brought under bondage to the rudiments of the world nor the consciences of other people. His attitude toward everyone and everything is one of good-natured tolerance if he does not like it, or smiling approval if he does. The things he does not like he is sure to pray about, and the things he approves he is sure to make matters of thanksgiving to God. But always he is relaxed and free from strain. He will not allow himself to get righteously upset about anything. "I lie near to the heart of God," he says, "and I fear nothing in the world."

The Christian Book of Mystical Verse
A. W. Tozer

The purpose of this book is to bring together in one convenient volume some of the best devotional verse the English language affords, and thus to make available to present day Christians a rich spiritual heritage which the greater number of them for various reasons do not now enjoy.

The Menace of the Religious Movie
A. W. Tozer

"Within the last few years a new method has been invented for imparting spiritual knowledge; or, to be more accurate, it is not new at all, but is an adaptation of a gadget of some years standing, one which by its origin and background belongs not to the Church but to the world. Some within the fold of the Church have thrown their mantle over it, have "blessed it with a text" and are now trying to show that it is the very gift of God for our day. But, however eloquent the sales talk, it is an unauthorized addition nevertheless, and was never a part of the pattern shown us on the mount.

Total Commitment to Christ: What is it?
A. W. Tozer

Tozer was a modern day prophet. His call to the Church was unequivocal: We must put Christ at the center of our lives and live for him and through him alone. He was an iconoclast among Evangelicals. One who sought to please God and not man. In this way he made many friends and many enemies. But everything that drove him was for the betterment of the human race in general and the Church in particular.

We have a growing selection of titles in print and eBook
All available on the Amazon and Createspace stores
Just search for CrossReach Publications!

Made in the USA
Monee, IL
06 January 2023

24611040R00016